Watkins

by Iain Gray

79 Main Street, Newtongrange,
Midlothian EH22 4NA
Tel: 0131 344 0414   Fax: 0845 075 6085
E-mail: info@lang-syne.co.uk
www.langsyneshop.co.uk

Design by Dorothy Meikle
Printed by Printwell Ltd
© Lang Syne Publishers Ltd 2020

All rights reserved. No part of this publication may be reproduced, stored or introduced into a retrieval system, or transmitted in any form or by any means (electronic, mechanical, photocopying, recording or otherwise) without the prior written permission of Lang Syne Publishers Ltd.

ISBN 978-1-85217-674-7

Watkins

MOTTOES include:
A golden head and true heart
(and)
Virtue is the way.

CRESTS include:
The head of a dragon
(and)
The head of a griffin.

NAME variations include:
Watkens
Watkin
Watkyns

Chapter one:

Origins of Welsh surnames

by Iain Gray

***If you don't know where you came from, you won't know where you're going* is a frequently quoted observation and one that has a particular resonance today when there has been a marked upsurge in interest in genealogy, with increasing numbers of people curious to trace their family roots.**

Main sources for genealogical research include census returns and official records of births, marriages and deaths – and the key to unlocking the detail they contain is obviously a family surname, one that has been 'inherited' and passed from generation to generation.

No matter our station in life, we all have a surname – but it was not until about the middle of the fourteenth century that the practice of being identified by a particular, or 'fixed', surname became commonly established throughout the British Isles.

Previous to this, it was normal for a person to be identified through the use of only a forename.

Wales, however, known in the Welsh language as *Cymru*, is uniquely different – with the use of what are known as patronymic names continuing well into the fifteenth century and, in remote rural areas, up until the early nineteenth century.

Patronymic names are ones where a son takes his father's forename, or Christian name, as his surname.

Examples of patronymic names throughout the British Isles include 'Johnson', indicating 'son of John', while specifically in Scotland 'son of' was denoted by the prefix Mc or Mac – with 'MacDonald', for example, meaning 'son of Donald.'

Early Welsh law, known as *Cyfraith Hywel*, *The Law of Hywel*, introduced by Hywel the Good, who ruled from Prestatyn to Pembroke between 915 AD and 950 AD, stipulated that a person's name should indicate their ancestry – the name in effect being a type of 'family tree.'

This required the prefixes *ap* or *ab* – derived from *mab*, meaning 'son of' being placed before the person's baptismal name.

In the case of females, the suffixes *verch* or *ferch*, sometimes shortened to *vch* or *vz* would be attached to their Christian name to indicate 'daughter of.'

In some cases, rather than being known for

example as *Llewellyn ap Thomas* – *Llewellyn son of Thomas* – Llewellyn's name would incorporate an 'ancestral tree' going back much earlier than his father.

One source gives the example of *Llewellyn ap Thomas ap Dafydd ap Evan ap Owen ap John* – meaning *Llewellyn son of Thomas son of Dafydd son of Evan son of Owen son of John*.

This leads to great confusion, to say the least, when trying to trace a person's ancestry back to a particular family – with many people having the forenames, for example, of Llewellyn, Thomas, Owen or John.

The first Act of Union between Wales and England that took place in 1536 during the reign of Henry VIII required that all Welsh names be registered in an Anglicised form – with *Hywel*, for example, becoming Howell, or Powell, and *Gruffydd* becoming Griffiths.

An early historical example of this concerns William ap John Thomas, standard bearer to Henry VIII, who became William Jones.

In many cases – as in Davies and Williams – an s was simply added to the original patronymic name, while in other cases the prefix *ap* or *ab* was contracted to *p* or *b* to prefix the name – as in *ab Evan* to form Bevan and *ap Richard* to form Pritchard.

Other original Welsh surnames – such as Morgan, originally *Morcant* – derive from ancient Celtic sources, while others stem from a person's physical characteristics – as in *Gwyn* or *Wynne* a nickname for someone with fair hair, *Gough* or *Gooch* denoting someone with red hair or a ruddy complexion, *Gethin* indicating swarthy or ugly and *Lloyd* someone with brown or grey hair.

With many popular surnames found today in Wales being based on popular Christian names such as John, this means that what is known as the 'stock' or 'pool' of names is comparatively small compared to that of common surnames found in England, Scotland and Ireland.

This explains why, in a typical Welsh village or town with many bearers of a particular name not necessarily being related, they were differentiated by being known, for example, as 'Jones the butcher', 'Jones the teacher' and 'Jones the grocer.'

Another common practice, dating from about the nineteenth century, was to differentiate among families of the same name by prefixing it with the mother's surname or hyphenating the name.

The history of the origins and development of Welsh surnames is inextricably bound up with the nation's frequently turbulent history and its rich culture.

Speaking a Celtic language known as Brythonic, which would gradually evolve into Welsh, the natives were subjected to Roman invasion in 48 AD, and in the following centuries to invasion by the Anglo-Saxons, Vikings and Normans.

Under England's ruthless and ambitious Edward I, the nation was fortified with castles between 1276 and 1295 to keep the 'rebellious' natives in check – but this did not prevent a series of bloody uprisings against English rule that included, most notably, Owain Glyndŵr's rebellion in 1400.

Politically united with England through the first Act of Union in 1536, becoming part of the Kingdom of Great Britain in 1707 and part of the United Kingdom in 1801, it was in 1999 that *Cynulliad Cenedlaethol Cymru*, the National Assembly for Wales, was officially opened by the Queen.

Welsh language and literature has flourished throughout the nation's long history.

In what is known as the Heroic Age, early Welsh poets include the late sixth century Taliesin and Aneirin, author of *Y Gododdin*.

Discovered in a thirteenth century manuscript but thought to date from anywhere between the seventh and eleventh centuries, it refers to the kingdom of Gododdin that took in south-east Scotland and

Northumberland and was part of what was once the Welsh territory known as *Hen Ogledd*, *The Old North*.

Commemorating Gododdin warriors who were killed in battle against the Angles of Bernicia and Deira at Catraith in about 600 AD, the manuscript – known as *Llyfr Aneirin*, *Book of Aneirin* – is now in the precious care of Cardiff City Library.

Other important early works by Welsh poets include the fourteenth century *Red Book of Hergest*, now held in the Bodleian Library, Oxford, and the *White Book of Rhydderch*, kept in the National Library of Wales, Aberystwyth.

William Morgan's translation of the Bible into Welsh in 1588 is hailed as having played an important role in the advancement of the Welsh language, while in 1885 Dan Isaac Davies founded the first Welsh language society.

It was in 1856 that Evan James and his son James James composed the rousing Welsh national anthem *Hen Wlad Fynhadad – Land of My Fathers*, while in the twentieth century the poet Dylan Thomas gained international fame and acclaim with poems such as *Under Milk Wood*.

The nation's proud cultural heritage is also celebrated through *Eisteddfod Genedlaethol Cymru*, the National Eisteddfod of Wales, the annual festival of music, literature and performance that is held across the nation and which traces its roots back to 1176 when Rhys ap Gruffyd, who ruled the territory of Deheubarth from 1155 to 1197, hosted a magnificent festival of poetry and song at his court in Cardigan.

The 2011 census for Wales unfortunately shows that the number of people able to speak the language has declined from 20.8% of the population of just under 3.1 million in 2001 to 19% – but overall the nation's proud culture, reflected in its surnames, still flourishes.

Many Welsh families proudly boast the heraldic device known as a Coat of Arms, as featured on our front cover.

The central motif of the Coat of Arms would originally have been what was borne on the shield of a warrior to distinguish himself from others on the battlefield.

Not featured on the Coat of Arms, but highlighted on page three, is the family motto and related crest – with the latter frequently different from the central motif.

Echoes of a far distant past can still be found in our surnames and they can be borne with pride in commemoration of our forebears.

Chapter two:

Ancient Britons

A patronymic surname, with the final 's' denoting 'son of', 'Watkins' ultimately derives from the Germanic given name 'Waldhar', meaning 'people-rule', while the English form is 'Walter.'

The forenames 'Wat' and 'Watt', meanwhile, are 'pet forms', or diminutives, of 'Walter' and were both popular Middle English names – and it is from these forms of the original Germanic 'Waldhar' that the Watkins surname stems.

With the forenames enjoying popularity in not only England but also in Wales centuries before the Norman Conquest of 1066, this means that flowing through the veins of many bearers of the Watkins name today is not only the blood of the original native Britons but also that of Anglo-Saxon, Viking and Norman invaders.

In Wales, the early heartland of those who would come to bear the Watkins name was the ancient kingdom of Brycheiniog, now modern-day Breconshire – one of the nation's thirteen historic counties and also known as Brecknockshire, County of Brecon, County of Brecknock and, in Welsh, as *Sir Frycheiniog* – with 'Sir' denoting 'County'.

Long before the Conquest, meanwhile, the ancestors of those who would assume the Watkins surname are believed to have held a family seat at Pennoyre, in Breconshire and, after the Conquest, were also established in the same county at Llangorse.

The first serious threat to the kingdom of Brycheiniog's independence came in the sixth century in the form of the Anglo-Saxons - those Germanic tribes who invaded and settled in the south and east of the island of Britain from about the early fifth century.

Composed of the Jutes, from the area of the Jutland Peninsula in modern Denmark, the Saxons from Lower Saxony and the Angles from the Angeln area of Germany, it was the latter who gave the name 'Engla land', or 'Aengla land' – better known as 'England.'

The Anglo-Saxons meanwhile, had usurped the power of the indigenous Britons, who referred to them as 'Saeson' or 'Saxones' – and it is from this that the Welsh term for English people of 'Saeson' derives, the Scottish-Gaelic 'Sasannach' and the Irish-Gaelic 'Sasanach.'

We learn from the *Anglo-Saxon Chronicle* how the religion of the early Anglo-Saxons was one that pre-dated the establishment of Christianity in the British Isles by about 690 A.D.

But, as a form of Germanic paganism with

roots in Old Norse religion, it shared much in common with the Druidic 'nature-worshipping' religion of the indigenous Britons such as the Welsh.

The first serious shock to Anglo-Saxon control came in 789 in the form of sinister black-sailed Viking ships that appeared over the horizon off the island monastery of Lindisfarne, in the northeast of England.

Lindisfarne was sacked in an orgy of violence and plunder, setting the scene for what would be many more terrifying raids on the coastline of not only England, but also of Wales, Ireland and Scotland.

Further invasion followed between approximately 950 AD and 1000 by the feared Northmen, and the coastline of Wales was repeatedly subjected to their raids – but, when not raping and pillaging, they established trading posts and settlements at modern day Haverfordwest, Fishguard and Caldey Island.

Through intermarriage, the bloodlines of the native Britons such as the Welsh became infused with those of the Anglo-Saxons and the Vikings.

But there would be another infusion of the blood of the 'Northmen' in the wake of the Norman Conquest of 1066 – a key event in the history of the British Isles that sounded the death knell of Anglo-Saxon supremacy and also Welsh independence.

This was when Harold II, last of the Anglo-

Saxon kings, was defeated at the battle of Hastings, in East Sussex, in October of that year by a mighty invasion force led by Duke William II of Normandy.

William was declared King of England on December 25, and the complete subjugation of his Anglo-Saxon subjects followed, with those Normans who had fought on his behalf rewarded with lands – a pattern that would be followed in Wales.

Invading across the Welsh Marches, the borderland between England and Wales, the Normans gradually consolidated their gains.

But, under a succession of Welsh leaders who included Llywelyn ap Gruffudd, known as Llywelyn the Last, resistance proved strong.

But Llwelyn's resistance was brutally crushed in 1283 under England's ruthless and ambitious Edward I, who ordered the building or repair of at least 17 castles and in 1302 proclaimed his son and heir, the future Edward II, as Prince of Wales, a title known in Welsh as *Tywysog Cymru*.

Another heroic Welsh figure dominated the resistance movement from 1400 to 1415 in the form of Owain Glyndŵr – the last native Welshman to be recognised by his supporters as *Tywysog Cymru*.

In what is known as The Welsh Revolt he achieved an early series of stunning victories against

Henry IV and his successor Henry V – until mysteriously disappearing from the historical record after mounting an ambush in Brecon.

Some sources assert that he was either killed in the ambush or died a short time afterwards from wounds he received – but there is a persistent tradition that he survived and lived thereafter in anonymity, protected by loyal followers.

During the revolt, he had consistently refused offers of a Royal Pardon and – despite offers of hefty rewards for his capture – he was never betrayed.

In the twentieth century, fascinated by Britain's ancient and mysterious past and the lives of the very early Britons such as the native Welsh, Alfred Watkins was the amateur archaeologist, antiquarian, photographer, author and businessman who in the early 1920s proposed the existence of what he termed 'ley lines.'

It had been while standing on a hill in his native Herefordshire that he noticed outlines of straight tracks that appeared to pass through landscape features such as burial mounds and hills where beacons would have been placed.

Subsequently travelling throughout the length and breadth of Herefordshire and spotting more ley lines – so named because many of the places where they passed through contained the syllable 'ley' – Watkins theorised they had first been laid down in Neolithic times to 'connect up' landscape features deemed sacred.

His theory was expounded in his 1922 book *Early British Trackways* and further elaborated upon in his 1925 *The old straight track: its mounds, beacons, moats, sites, and mark stones*, while they were expanded upon in the 1960s by, for example, John Michell in his book *The View Over Atlantis*.

A member of the Old Straight Track Club from its foundation in 1927, a member of the Society for the Protection of Ancient Buildings and, as a respected photographer, a Fellow of the Royal Photographic Society, he died in 1935.

Chapter three:

Poetry and politics

A close friend of fellow Welshman the great poet Dylan Thomas, Vernon Watkins was also an acclaimed poet – praised by Thomas as "the most profound and greatly accomplished Welshman writing poems in English."

Also a translator and painter, he was born in 1906 in Maesteg, Glamorgan but raised mainly in Swansea.

Somewhat of a child prodigy, he was able to read fluently by the time he was aged only four – rather precociously announcing to his bemused parents a year later that he wanted to be a poet, but not to be published until after his death.

Educated at private schools in Sussex and Derbyshire, he studied modern languages at Cambridge University but dropped out before completing his degree.

Finding employment with a bank in Swansea, he first met Dylan Thomas in 1935, with the latter a regular visitor to the Watkins family home located at the top of the cliffs of the Gower peninsula.

It was an odd friendship – with Thomas leading

a chaotic and frequently inebriated lifestyle while Watkins was decidedly more organised.

But Watkins was the only person whose advice Thomas sought when writing his poetry and often the first he allowed to read his finished work.

During the Second World War Watkins worked as a cryptographer at Bletchley Park, Buckinghamshire, where German radio traffic was decoded, and it was here that he met his future wife Gwen.

The couple married in 1944 and, in typical disorganised fashion, Watkins' best man, his friend Dylan, failed to turn up for the ceremony – but this did not affect their friendship.

Watkins becoming godfather to Thomas's son Llewelyn, while he also wrote the poet's obituary when the author of noted works that include *Fern Hill*, *Under Milk Wood*, *Do not go gentle into that good night* and *Death shall have no dominion* died after a drunken binge in November of 1953 in New York while on a series of reading tours and radio broadcasts.

Having still dedicated himself to his poetry during the war years while also working as a cryptographer, Watkins' first collection of poetry – *Ballad of the Mari Llwyd* – was published by *Faber and Faber* in 1941 and he became associated with the New Apocalyptics group of poets.

Returning to work with the bank in Swansea, he was known to spend several hours every night when he returned from work immersed in the art of poetic creation.

Awarded a University of Wales honorary doctorate in 1966, he died a year later.

In common with his great friend Dylan Thomas, this was also in the United States – in his case while playing tennis in Seattle, where he had been a guest teacher on modern poetry at the University of Washington.

His body returned to his native Wales, he was buried in the Gower, St Mary's Church, Pennard, near Swansea, while a granite memorial to him was erected at Hunt's Bay, Gower.

It is inscribed with the poignant line from his poem *Taliesin in Gower*:

*I have been taught the script of stones,
and I know the tongue of the wave*

A portrait of him is held by the Glynn Vivian Art Gallery, Swansea, while in a 2012 BBC Radio 3 programme, *Swansea's Other Poet*, the then Archbishop of Canterbury and fellow Welshman Dr Rowan Williams paid tribute to him as "one of the twentieth century's most brilliant and distinctive yet unjustly neglected voices."

From poetry to the much different world of politics, Elwyn Watkins, more formally known as Baron Watkins of Glantane, was the Welsh senior Labour Party politician born in 1903 at Abercrave, in the Swansea Valley.

The son of a local councillor and lay preacher, he was aged just under 14 when he first entered the dark and dangerous bowels of the earth as a coalminer.

Exhausted after his day's labours, he nevertheless found time to educate himself through the Workers' Educational Association (WEA) and the National Council of Labour Colleges.

Working in the mines until he was aged 22, he later became the Labour Party agent for the Brecon and Radnor constituency – and from 1945 until he retired from the Commons in 1970, Member of Parliament (MP) for the constituency.

Along with four other Welsh Labour MPs, he broke with party directive by passionately arguing for a Welsh Parliament, while from 1964 to 1966 he served as Parliamentary Private Secretary (PPS) to James Griffiths, the first Secretary of State for Wales, and then to his successor Cledwyn Hughes.

A prominent Welsh member of the Commons, he served from 1966 to 1968 as chairman of the Parliamentary Select Committee on Agriculture in addition to a number of bodies that included the Wales Tourist Board, the Civil Aviation Advisory Committee for Wales, the Welsh Panel of the British Council and the Mid-Wales Industrial Development Association.

Created Baron Watkins of Glantane in 1972, he became active in local government – serving in posts that included chairman of Breconshire County Council and, from 1974 to 1977, the first chairman of the newly-created Powys County Council and, from 1975 to 1978, Lord Lieutenant of Powys.

Also chairman for a time of the Brecon Beacons National Park Committee, he died in 1983.

With the popular Watkins spelling variation of 'Watkin', Professor Thomas Glyn Watkin is the Welsh lawyer who, in 2007, became the first person appointed to the post of First Legislative Counsel to the Welsh Government.

Born in 1952 in Cwmparc, in the Rhondda Valley and appointed foundation professor of law at the University of Wales, Bangor, in 2004 and an expert in both civil law and legal history and an ordained priest in the Church of Wales, his many publications include his 1980 *The Nature of Law* and, from 2005, *Wales: An Introduction to Its Legal History*.

Responsible for coining journalistic phrases

that have entered into common parlance, Alan Watkins was the Welsh columnist for newspaper and magazines born in 1933 in Tycroes, Carmarthenshire.

He qualified as a lawyer, but turning his back on a career in the legal profession he found himself in London's Fleet Street – where for more than 50 years he was a political commentator for newspapers that included *The Observer*, the *Sunday Mirror*, *Sunday Express* and *London Evening Standard*.

From 1964 to 1967 he also contributed to *The Spectator* magazine, while from 1967 until 1976 he worked for the *New Statesman*.

It was in May of 1990, during the ultimately successful attempt by senior Conservative Party figures to persuade their leader Prime Minister Margaret Thatcher to resign, that he described them as "the men in suits."

This subsequently became reported and since quoted as "the men in grey suits."

Another of the frequently quoted phrases he coined is "young fogeys" – descriptive of young politicians who strive to attain some gravitas by adopting the air of, and perhaps even dressing as, someone much older.

Author of a number of books that include his 1991 *A Conservative Coup: The Fall of Margaret Thatcher* and, from 2000, the autobiographical *A Short Walk Down Fleet Street*, he died in 2010.

From politics to the battlefield, Sir Tasker Watkins was not only a Welsh recipient of the Victoria Cross – the highest award for gallantry in the face of enemy action for British and Commonwealth forces – but also a prominent judge and an official of the Welsh Rugby Union.

Born in 1918 in Nelson, Glamorgan, he entered the army as a private on the outbreak of war and was commissioned into the Welch Regiment in 1941 as a lieutenant. In August of 1944, at Barfour, Normandy, in the aftermath of the D-Day landings and the only officer left from his unit, he led a bayonet charge against enemy infantry and single-handedly silenced a machine-gun post.

Later promoted to the rank of major, he studied law when the conflict ended.

Called to the bar in 1948 and appointed a Queen's Counsel (QC) in 1965, he was appointed to the High Court bench six years later and knighted.

Other top judicial positions followed and, in 1988, he was appointed Deputy Chief Justice.

A passionate rugby supporter and having played for the army, Glamorgan Wanderers and Cardiff, he served from 1993 to 2004 as president of the Welsh Rugby Union.

Also chairman, president and a patron of Glamorgan Wanderers until his death in 2007, he is honoured by a statue in its club house, while another stands outside Gate C in the Millennium stadium, Cardiff.

His VC is now on display at the Imperial War Museum, London.

Chapter four:

On the world stage

An award-winning English actor of stage, television and film, Jason Watkins was born in 1963.

On stage, his performance at London's Old Vic in a production of *A Servant for Two Masters* won him a nomination in 2001 for a Laurence Olivier Theatre Award for Best Supporting Actor, while his many television credits include that of the vampire leader Will Herrick in *Being Human* and of Pornich in the 2008 BBC production of Charles Dickens' *Little Dorrit*.

Winner of a BAFTA for Best Actor in 2014 for his leading role in the drama *The Lost Honour of Christopher Jeffries*, other television credits include *Lark Rise to Candleford*, *Life on Mars*, the comedy *Psychoville*, *Dirk Gently* and the sitcom *Trollied*, while big screen credits include the 2006 *Confetti* and, from 2008, *Wild Child*.

Behind the camera lens, **James Watkins** is the British film director and screenwriter born in Nottingham in 1973.

As a director, he is best known for the 2012 *The Woman in Black*, starring *Harry Potter* lead actor Daniel Radcliffe and the 2015 *Bastille Day*, while as both a writer and a director his 2008 *Eden Lake*, starring Michael Fassbender and Kelly Reilly, won best Horror Film at the *Empire* Awards.

Nominated for the Douglas Hickox Award at the 2008 British Independent Film awards, his other screenwriting credits include the 2002 *My Little Eye* and, from 2009, *The Descent Part 2*.

Recognised as one of the pioneers of the film genre known as docudrama, **Peter Watkins** is the English television and film director born in 1935 in Norbiton, Surrey.

Portraying real historical events or imagined events from the future with the actors being followed by camera crews and interviewed by news reporters, the docudrama technique was first employed by Watkins in his 1964 television film *Culloden* – charting the abortive Jacobite Rising of 1745.

Winner of a Jacob's Award for *Culloden*, he also successfully employed the technique in *La Commune*, depicting the events surrounding the 1871 revolutionary movement known as the Paris Commune.

Following the critical acclaim for *Culloden*, Watkins was commissioned by the BBC in 1965 for *The War Game* – a docudrama depicting a future nuclear war and its aftermath.

But, deemed too harrowing for viewers, it was

shelved by the BBC and not screened on television until 20 years later.

It was, however, released to cinemas and went on to win the 1966 Academy Award for Best Documentary Feature.

Born in 1896 in Louisville, Kentucky, **Maurine Dallas Watkins** was the American journalist, playwright and screenwriter whose most successful play, *Chicago*, enjoyed success after her death as a musical and, later, as a film.

Joining the staff of the *Chicago Tribune* in 1924 as a news reporter, she wrote a fictionalised account of a double-murder she had covered and named it *The Brave Little Woman* – later changing the title to *Chicago*.

It had success as a play and Watkins went on to Hollywood, where she wrote a number of screenplays that include the 1936 comedy *Libeled Lady*, starring Spencer Tracy, Jean Harlow and Myrna Lloyd.

Shortly before her death in 1966, she was approached by the musical theatre choreographer and director Bob Fosse who offered to buy the rights to *Chicago* to adapt it for a stage musical.

She refused, but following her death her estate sold the rights and *Chicago: A Musical Vaudeville*, was first staged in 1975; revived again for the stage in 1997, it was filmed as *Chicago* in 2002.

In contemporary music, **Ian "H" Watkins** is the Welsh singer, dancer and actor best known as a member of the pop group Steps.

Born in 1976 in Llwynpa, Mid-Glamorgan, Watkins, who has said the "H" in his name stands for "hyperactive", formed a duo with former Steps member Claire Richards when the group split up.

The subject of a reality television series, *H-side story*, he received the rather dubious accolade of being placed at No. 8 in a 2003 Channel 4 poll of "100 Worst Britons We Love to Hate."

Lead singer in the 1990s with the internationally successful rhythm and blues and hip-hop girl-band TLC, Tionne Tenese Watkins is the American singer, songwriter, dancer and actress better known by her stage name **T-Boz**.

Born in 1970 in Des Moines, Iowa she was the recipient of four Grammy Awards with TLC, while as a solo artist her single *Touch Myself* was used on the soundtrack of the 1996 film *Fled*, while *My Getaway* was used in the 2000 *Rugrats in Paris: The Movie*.

As an actress, her film credits include the 1998 *Belly* while, having revealed that she suffers from Sickle Cell Disease, she is a leading spokesperson and fundraiser for Sickle Cell Disease Association of America.

Bearers of the Watkins name have also excelled in the highly competitive world of sport – not least in the rough and tumble that is the Welsh national game of rugby.

The recipient of an MBE for his services to the game, **David Watkins** is the former dual-code Welsh rugby union international who played both rugby union and rugby league for his native Wales and for Great Britain between 1963 and 1974.

Born in 1942 in Blaina, South Wales, and having captained the British and Irish Lions rugby union side, he played at club level for teams that include Newport and Pontypool.

Coach for a time of both the Wales national team and Great Britain, he was installed as a patron of the Welsh Rugby Union in 2006 in a special ceremony in the National Assembly for Wales, while in 2009 he was appointed president of Crusaders.

A Welsh former international rugby union wing, **Stuart Watkins** was born in Newport in 1941.

Representing his nation on no fewer than 26 occasions, making his debut in a winning game against Scotland in 1964 and having played club rugby for Cardiff and Newport, he was also selected in 1966 to play for the British Lions on their tour of Australia and New Zealand.

Born in Ebbw Vale in 1962, **Ian Watkins** is the Welsh former international rugby union player capped ten times for his nation and who played at club level for Ebbw Vale and Cardiff.

Still on the rugby pitch, Matthew Watkins, also referred to as **Matthew J. Watkins** to distinguish him from another player of the name, is the Welsh international rugby union centre born in Newport in 1978 and who played at club level for Newbridge, Ponllanfraith, Newport and Llanelli; at regional level, he also played for teams that include Llanelli Scarlets.

Welsh bearers of the Watkins name have also excelled on the cricket pitch.

Born in Usk, Monmouthshire in 1922, Albert John Watkins was the all-rounder better known as **Allan Watkins**.

Making his debut for Glamorgan shortly before the outbreak of the Second World War, he went on to play for the county until 1961.

Having played for England in fifteen Tests from 1948 to 1952 and the first Glamorgan cricketer to score a century in Tests for England, he died in 2011.

Born in Abergavenny in 1983, **Ryan Watkins** is the cricketer who also played for Glamorgan and who holds the record by a Glamorgan outfielder for the most catches in a match – this was seven, in a County

Championship match against Kent County Cricket Club.

Another cricketer for Glamorgan, albeit for a brief spell in 1950, was **Bill Watkins**, born in Swansea in 1923.

He served in the RAF during the Second World War and was involved in 31 bombing missions over Germany, earning him the Distinguished Flying Cross (DFC); he died in 2005.

From sport to photography, **John Watkins**, born in 1823 and who died in 1874, was the English portrait photographer who, sometimes in collaboration with his brother Octavius, captured the images of famous Victorian figures including Charles Dickens, the Prince of Wales and the philosopher John Stuart Mill.

One bearer of the proud name of Watkins whose legacy survives to this day in the form of a number of popular comic strips was the English cartoonist and illustrator Dudley Dexter Watkins, better known as **Dudley D. Watkins**.

Born in 1907 in Prestwich, Lancashire and moving as a child with his family to Nottingham, his father – a lithographic printer   recognised his artistic talents from an early age and arranged for him to attend art classes at Nottingham School of Art.

Later studying full-time at the school, he

enrolled in Glasgow School of Art in 1924 and, a year later and on the recommendation of the school's principal, found employment as an illustrator with the Dundee-based publishers D.C. Thomson.

From providing illustrations for boys' papers that included *Rover*, *Wizard* and *Hotspur*, he later became better known for his comic strip characters *The Broons* and *Oor Wullie* – co-created with the editor and writer R.D. Low and which have been a highly popular feature of D.C. Thomson's *Sunday Post* newspaper since 1936 along with their appearance in annual book format.

Also responsible for illustrating characters for comics that include *The Beano* and *The Dandy*, he worked right up until he was found dead at his drawing board in 1969.